Shannon Raises Puppies

for

Guide Dogs For the Blind

Shannon Raises Puppies

for

Guide Dogs For the Blind

by

Shannon Patterson and Diane Deaver

Shannon Raises Puppies for Guide Dogs for the Blind
Copyright © 2019 by Shannon Patterson and Diane Deaver

ISBN 978-1-935914-97-6

Design by River Sanctuary Graphic Arts

Printed in the United States of America

Additional copies available from:

www.riversanctuarypublishing.com
Amazon.com

River Sanctuary Publishing
P.O Box 1561
Felton, CA 95018
www.riversanctuarypublishing.com
Dedicated to the awakening of the New Earth

STANTON

Shannon was eight years old when she heard about Guide Dogs for the Blind. Her teacher brought a puppy to school and said she was raising him to hopefully help a blind person.

Shannon told her family about it that night. Her mother Pegeen was a veterinarian and helped animals. Her father Doug was a fireman and helped people and animals in fires and other emergencies. Her brother Nathan was five years old and liked animals. They had dogs, cats, horses, chickens, and fish and wanted to find out more about guide dog puppies.

Shannon and Stanton

Shannon and Pegeen went to meetings to find out more about raising a guide dog puppy, and the family decided they would like to do it.

The puppy truck delivered Stanton to a park near Shannon's house, and Shannon was very excited! Stanton was eight weeks old and was a yellow Labrador puppy. He had beautiful big brown eyes, loved to cuddle, and was very friendly. Yellow and black labs often make good guide dogs because they adjust well to many different people. The whole family loved him and felt he was a good addition to the family.

Stanton often wore a special vest which said "Guide Dogs for the Blind Puppy in Training," and that let people know he was working and shouldn't be distracted.

Stanton wearing his vest

Stanton learned he had to wait until his vest came off before he could go to the bathroom. That was his signal that he wasn't working. He wasn't allowed to play with a ball because it would be very dangerous to chase a ball into the street when he was guiding a blind person. He slept in a crate at night. He loved to sleep and was happy to curl up and take a nap and could sleep anywhere.

Shannon worked with Stanton for almost a year and a half, and then it was time for him to get tested to see if he could become a guide dog. Shannon and her family hoped he would pass the tests so he could help a blind person.

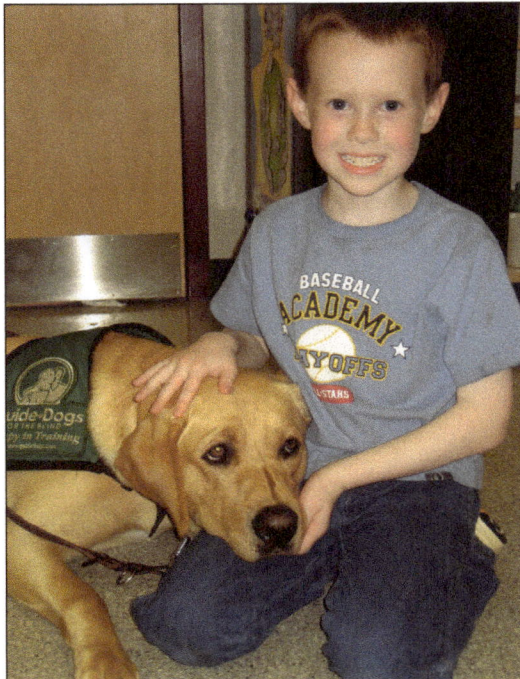

Stanton with Nathan

The puppy truck came back to the park in their town and picked up Stanton to take him back to the campus for Guide Dogs for the Blind for testing and training.

Shannon, Stanton, and Nathan with the puppy truck

First the dogs have a thorough medical exam. Then they go through much training, and each step of the training gets more difficult. They learn to deal with traffic, buses, trains, escalators, obedience, and obstacle training, and they need to pass all the tests to become a guide dog.

A few weeks later they got the news that Stanton had not passed every test. Shannon and her family could adopt him if they wished. They said yes, so he had a career change and became a family pet. Now instead of sleeping in a crate he slept in a cozy spot near Shannon's bed.

Shannon was disappointed that Stanton couldn't help a blind person, but she and her family loved him and enjoyed having him stay as part of their family.

Stanton in a cozy spot near Shannon's bed

EATON

The next dog Shannon was raising for Guide Dogs for the Blind was a black lab name Eaton. When the puppy van came to the park in town to pick up Stanton, it delivered Eaton at the same time. Eaton was 8 weeks old and very cute.

The puppy truck arrives with Eaton

Eaton adjusted to the leash and the vest. He learned to obey rules. Guide dogs in training go many places with their people so they get used to different noises, people, smells, and activities. They need to remain calm and not get too distracted. He sometimes went to school with Shannon for visits, and then Shannon's mom would take him home. He loved making new friends at school.

Eaton wearing his vest

Eaton snored when he slept. One time in Shannon's fifth grade class, he was snoring and the teacher was trying to figure out which student had fallen asleep while he was teaching. He finally turned around and asked, "Who is snoring?" and the students all said "It's the dog!" and laughed.

Eaton also went to the grocery store, the bank, and the hairdresser with Shannon's mom and went to many places with the family such as the lake.

Eaton at the lake with Shannon and Pegeen

After many months, Eaton went to the Guide Dogs for the Blind campus to see if he could become a guide dog. He passed all the tests. The family was very excited!

Eaton met Albert, a blind man, and a guide dog trainer helped Albert and Eaton learn to work together.

At last the day came when Shannon and her family would meet Albert and then Shannon would present Eaton to him and make a speech at graduation. It was an exciting day! Then it was time to say goodbye to Eaton. Shannon knew she would miss him but he had an important job to do and it made her happy that he could help Albert. Albert lived in Northern California and they kept in touch after graduation. Shannon's family even took care of Eaton for a few weeks a few years later when Albert went on a trip and didn't want to take Eaton.

Eaton at Graduation

KIPLING

Next Shannon raised Kipling, a puppy who was three fourths golden retriever and one fourth yellow lab. He was very friendly and went many places, even to the Monterey Bay Aquarium. The family had to be sure no one stepped on his tail and hurt him when he was sitting down in the crowd. People always wanted to pet him, but they had to say he was working so he wouldn't be distracted when he was wearing his vest.

Shannon and Kipling

Kipling had a serious working face, so people often thought he was sad, but he was just focused. Since he was mostly golden retriever, he was a little more fluffy than the other dogs.

When the puppies were not wearing the vest and were not working, they were still required to have good house manners but were able to be playful puppies.

Kipling at the beach

Kipling at a friend's pool

Kipling at the fire station

After many months, Kipling went for testing and unfortunately, he didn't pass every test. About half of the puppies raised for Guide Dogs for the Blind pass all of the tests and become guide dogs. Kipling went to live with a close family friend who had seen Kipling many times and was impressed with what a good dog he was.

Kipling enjoying the outdoors

ALBUS

Shannon's next puppy was Albus, a yellow lab. Albus was another friendly puppy who came to Shannon when he was eight weeks old. That's the age the puppies are when they can leave their mother and come to a family. The puppy truck delivered Albus to the park.

Shannon and Nathan meeting Albus

Albus was very easy to house train and was always very reliable and confident in public. He could handle any distraction and situation Shannon and her family encountered with him. People often thought his name was "Elvis" if Shannon said his name too fast.

Albus enjoyed celebrating holidays with the family.

Shannon and Albus at Halloween

Albus celebrating Christmas

Shannon graduated from 8th grade and Albus went with her to graduation and walked across the stage with her.

Shannon and Albus the day of Shannon's 8th grade graduation

After Albus was with Shannon and her family for about a year and a half, he returned to Guide Dogs for the Blind and passed all of the tests.

Another graduation took place! Shannon presented Reg with Albus, and he was thrilled. He lives in Canada, and Shannon and all of her family are still in touch with him. Albus had to get used to wearing booties in the snow in the winter to protect his feet from the cold since it gets very cold there. Reg has invited Shannon's family to visit sometime, and they hope to be able to someday.

Albus

KING

Shannon's next puppy was King, a black lab. Some guide dog puppies are female, but Shannon's family requested all males.

Shannon greeting King

King adjusted well to the family.

King enjoying all the other dogs in the family

King was goofy and clumsy and loved meeting new people. He was always happy, and his tail wagged wherever he would go.

Shannon enjoyed many activities with each dog that she raised.

Shannon and King playing in the pool

King did not pass all the tests, and Shannon and her family kept him. He had a career change and became a family pet.

Shannon missed all of the dogs she had raised and who were either working dogs or with another family, but she was still in touch with their families and was proud that two of them were working dogs and making a blind person's life much better.

J.J.

Shannon's next dog was J.J., a yellow lab. All of the dogs in one litter have a name that starts with the same letter. Shannon always heard what the letter was before she got the puppy, and she would try to guess what the name might be.

Shannon and J.J.

She co-raised J.J. with another family so she had him half of the time. He adjusted well to the vest, the rules, and being shared by two families. J.J. loved to get belly rubs.

He liked to cuddle with the other dogs and take naps with them. If Shannon was in public with J.J. and she let someone pet him, he would lie on his back. It was cute, but it was embarrassing in the middle of a store.

When J.J. got tested about a year and a half later, he passed all of the tests! Another dog would graduate from Guide Dogs for the Blind and help a blind person! Shannon and her family met Gregory who lives in Canada and they keep in touch with him. They are happy to know what happens to all the dogs after they leave the family.

Gregory, J.J., Shannon, Nathan, and co-raisers at graduation at Guide Dogs for the Blind

Shannon has graduated from high school and is currently in college, so she won't be raising puppies for a while. She and her family have made a wonderful contribution to three blind people, making their lives much fuller and more independent by having a guide dog. It has been quite an adventure and has enriched Shannon and her family's lives for the last nine years.

Shannon graduating from High School

A VERY SPECIAL GIFT

She works with guide dog puppies
Works for hours every day
To socialize the animals
And teach them to obey.

She has some rules to follow
For eighteen months or so
She trains them to be well behaved
And friendly as they grow.

The dogs then go for testing
To see if they are right
To be paired with someone who is blind
A guide to be their sight.

Then Shannon waits to see if they
Are equal to the tasks
And when one passes, she is thrilled
To help is all she asks.

She's raised so far six puppies
And three have passed the test
And live to help someone who's blind
The dogs are just the best.

Such a gift to give these people
A great dog to help them see
And Shannon feels rewarded
To help the blind feel free.

Poem written for Shannon by Diane Deaver